Instant Cartoons for Church Newsletters

George W. Knight *Compiler*

BAKER BOOK HOUSE
Grand Rapids, Michigan 49516

Copyright 1988 by Baker Book House Company

ISBN: 0-8010-5492-3

Third printing, May 1990

Printed in the United States of America

Another Handy Book of Tasteful Church Humor: A New Compilation

All three of the previous books in this series—Instant Cartoons #1, 2, and 3—are alive and well, with churches asking for more. I'm delighted to respond to this continuing need by issuing Instant Cartoons #4.

This book introduces the work of two new cartoonists to this series—Doug Jones of Nashville, Tennessee, and Louis Goodwin of Columbus, Ohio. Many of Doug's cartoons have a youth slant, making them suitable for use in youth newsletters as well as general church publications. Louis also has a style uniquely his own, which should bring some healthy chuckles to the readers of your church publications.

Judging from the continuing circulation of the books in this series, Christians do enjoy an occasional look at the lighter side of their faith. And let's face it, a cartoon is often the only thing that will attract some people to read the newsletter.

George W. Knight

About the Cartoonists . . .

Doug Jones of Nashville, Tennessee, has been drawing cartoons since he was old enough to hold a crayon. In addition to his work as a humorous illustrator for the Baptist Sunday School Board, he also does freelance cartooning and humorous illustration projects for a number of different clients.

Joe McKeever is pastor of the First Baptist Church of Charlotte, North Carolina. A member of the National Cartoonist's Society, he creates cartoons that appear regularly in Southern Baptist newspapers as well as several general religious publications.

Louis Goodwin served more than 25 years as editorial cartoonist for the Columbus, Ohio Dispatch, where he drew two feature comic strips. Now retired, he is a member of the Association of American Editorial Cartoonists. His freelance cartoons have appeared in several magazines and newspapers.

"AS TELEVISION PREACHERS GO, HE'S NOT BAD! I JUST CAN'T STAND HIS 'AMEN-TRACK'!"

"THAT BALL DISAPPEARED LIKE DOCTRINAL CONTROVERSY AT A PRAYER MEETING!"

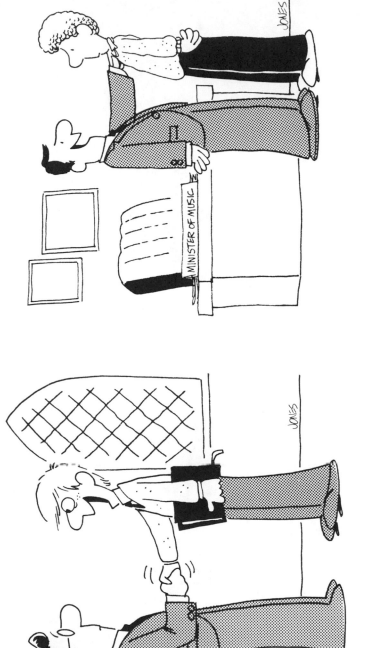

"OF COURSE YOU CAN JOIN THE CHOIR . . . NONE OF US SING ANYMORE, WE JUST LIP-SYNC TO TAPES!"

"WITH A LITTLE WORK, PASTOR, THAT SERMON ON SIN WOULD MAKE A GREAT TV MINI-SERIES!"

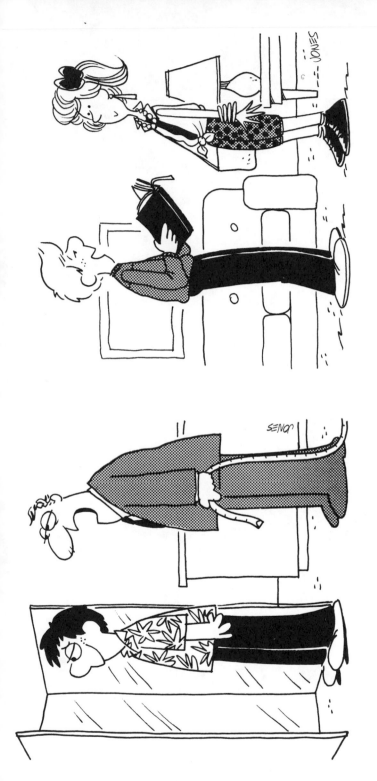

"YES, I'M SURE YOU'RE RIGHT. IF JOSEPH HAD SEEN THIS SHIRT, HE WOULD HAVE TRADED HIS COAT OF MANY COLORS FOR IT!"

"YOU CAN RELAX . . . THERE'S NOTHING IN LEVITICUS AGAINST HANGING OUT IN THE MALL!"

"WITH A LITTLE WORK, PASTOR, THAT
SERMON ON SIN WOULD MAKE A
GREAT TV MINI-SERIES!"

"OF COURSE YOU CAN JOIN THE
CHOIR . . . NONE OF US SING
ANYMORE, WE JUST LIP-SYNC
TO TAPES!"

"YES, I'M SURE YOU'RE RIGHT. IF
JOSEPH HAD SEEN THIS SHIRT, HE
WOULD HAVE TRADED HIS COAT OF
MANY COLORS FOR IT!"

"YOU CAN RELAX . . . THERE'S
NOTHING IN LEVITICUS AGAINST
HANGING OUT IN THE MALL!"

"I'M SORRY, DEAR, BUT YOUR REMOTE CONTROL DOESN'T WORK IN CHURCH!"

"I GUESS I SHOULD BE OUT WITNESSING MORE, BUT THERE ARE JUST SO MANY PROGRAMS ON CABLE TV I NEED TO WATCH!"

"AND THIS IS MY UNCLE HAROLD. HE DIDN'T BELIEVE IN DRINKING, DANCING, OR GOING TO MOVIES. HE LOST ALL OF HIS MONEY PLAYING BINGO!"

"SOME DAYS I JUST NEED A JUMP START!"

"I GUESS I SHOULD BE OUT WITNESSING MORE, BUT THERE ARE JUST SO MANY PROGRAMS ON CABLE TV I NEED TO WATCH!"

"I'M SORRY, DEAR, BUT YOUR REMOTE CONTROL DOESN'T WORK IN CHURCH!"

"AND THIS IS MY UNCLE HAROLD. HE DIDN'T BELIEVE IN DRINKING, DANCING, OR GOING TO MOVIES. HE LOST ALL OF HIS MONEY PLAYING BINGO!"

"SOME DAYS I JUST NEED A JUMP START!"

"I USED TO MEMORIZE SCRIPTURES, BUT I JUST DON'T HAVE THE TIME TO ANYMORE."

"ALL RIGHT . . . WHO PUT THE TURTLE IN THE BAPTISTRY?"

"WHY IS IT WE ONLY SING THE FIRST AND LAST VERSES OF OUR HYMNS, BUT WE SING ALL SIX VERSES OF THE INVITATION THROUGH TWICE?"

"I'M JUST TRYING TO GET A LITTLE DIFFERENT PERSPECTIVE ON THINGS!"

"ALL RIGHT . . . WHO PUT THE TURTLE
IN THE BAPTISTRY?"

"I USED TO MEMORIZE SCRIPTURES,
BUT I JUST DON'T HAVE THE TIME
TO ANYMORE."

"I'M JUST TRYING TO GET A LITTLE
DIFFERENT PERSPECTIVE ON THINGS!"

"WHY IS IT WE ONLY SING THE FIRST
AND LAST VERSES OF OUR HYMNS,
BUT WE SING ALL SIX VERSES OF THE
INVITATION THROUGH TWICE?"

"DO YOU HAVE ANY COMMUNION WAFERS THAT ARE NACHO CHEESE FLAVORED?"

"I'M GOING FOR THE WORLD'S RECORD ON HOW MANY BULLETINS I CAN COLLECT IN MY BIBLE!"

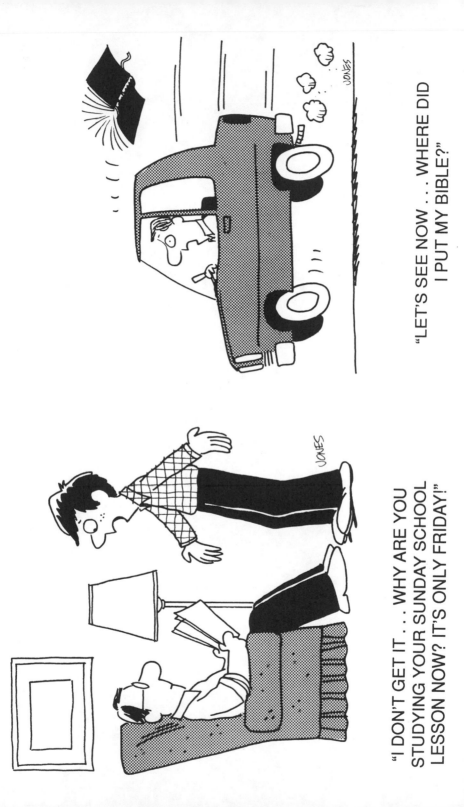

"I DON'T GET IT . . . WHY ARE YOU STUDYING YOUR SUNDAY SCHOOL LESSON NOW? IT'S ONLY FRIDAY!"

"LET'S SEE NOW . . . WHERE DID I PUT MY BIBLE?"

"I'M GOING FOR THE WORLD'S
RECORD ON HOW MANY BULLETINS
I CAN COLLECT IN MY BIBLE!"

"DO YOU HAVE ANY COMMUNION
WAFERS THAT ARE NACHO CHEESE
FLAVORED?"

"I DON'T GET IT . . . WHY ARE YOU
STUDYING YOUR SUNDAY SCHOOL
LESSON NOW? IT'S ONLY FRIDAY!"

"LET'S SEE NOW . . . WHERE DID
I PUT MY BIBLE?"

"NO. IT'S CALLED A BAPTISM . . . NOT A SLAM DUNK!"

"THIS BOOK IS OVERDUE? WELL, JUST TAKE THE FINE OUT OF MY TITHE."

"THIS BOOK IS OVERDUE? WELL, JUST TAKE THE FINE OUT OF MY TITHE."

"NO. IT'S CALLED A BAPTISM . . . NOT A SLAM DUNK!"

"IT'S A NICE LETTER, SUE, BUT IT'S NOT EVEN CLOSE TO HOW THE APOSTLE PAUL WOULD HAVE WRITTEN IT."

"I HAVE 6 CLASSICAL TAPES, 4 JAZZ TAPES, AND 38 CONTEMPORARY CHRISTIAN MUSIC TAPES. AM I SPIRITUAL OR WHAT?"

"SHE'S TRYING TO GET IN THE WORLD RECORD BOOK BY TALKING TILL SHE ACHIEVES TELEPHONE MELTDOWN!"

"I HAVE THE IMPRESSION THAT SOME OF YOU ARE NOT CONCENTRATING ON THE SERMON."

"BUT YOU DON'T UNDERSTAND . . . I'M LIKE SAMSON. GET RID OF MY HAIR, MAN, AND I'M NOTHIN'!"

"WELL, YES . . . I GUESS YOU COULD SAY JONAH TOOK THE FIRST SUBMARINE RIDE."

"I HAVE THE IMPRESSION THAT SOME OF YOU ARE NOT CONCENTRATING ON THE SERMON."

"SHE'S TRYING TO GET IN THE WORLD RECORD BOOK BY TALKING TILL SHE ACHIEVES TELEPHONE MELTDOWN!"

"BUT YOU DON'T UNDERSTAND . . . I'M LIKE SAMSON. GET RID OF MY HAIR, MAN, AND I'M NOTHIN'!"

"WELL, YES . . . I GUESS YOU COULD SAY JONAH TOOK THE FIRST SUBMARINE RIDE."

YOUTH SUNDAY SCHOOL

WELL, YES . . . IT IS HARD TO IMAGINE
THERE NOT BEING ANY HAMBURGER
STANDS AROUND IN PAUL'S DAY!"

"HAVEN'T YOU HEARD? RIGHT AFTER
THE SERVICE THERE'S GOING TO BE
AN ICE CREAM FELLOWSHIP!"

"JUST RELAX . . . I HAVEN'T LOST ANYONE IN A BAPTISM YET!"

"NO, NO. IN A RESTAURANT YOU LEAVE A TIP . . . NOT A TITHE!"

"HAVEN'T YOU HEARD? RIGHT AFTER
THE SERVICE THERE'S GOING TO BE
AN ICE CREAM FELLOWSHIP!"

WELL, YES . . . IT IS HARD TO IMAGINE
THERE NOT BEING ANY HAMBURGER
STANDS AROUND IN PAUL'S DAY!"

"NO, NO. IN A RESTAURANT YOU LEAVE
A TIP . . . NOT A TITHE!"

"JUST RELAX . . . I HAVEN'T LOST
ANYONE IN A BAPTISM YET!"

"WHEN IT'S TIME FOR THE OFFERING, I STICK THIS IN FRONT OF HIM. LAST WEEK I GOT FIVE DOLLARS!"

"DON'T BOTHER ME . . . I'M LOOKING FOR THE VERSE THAT SAYS IT'S OK FOR ME TO BORROW THE CAR."

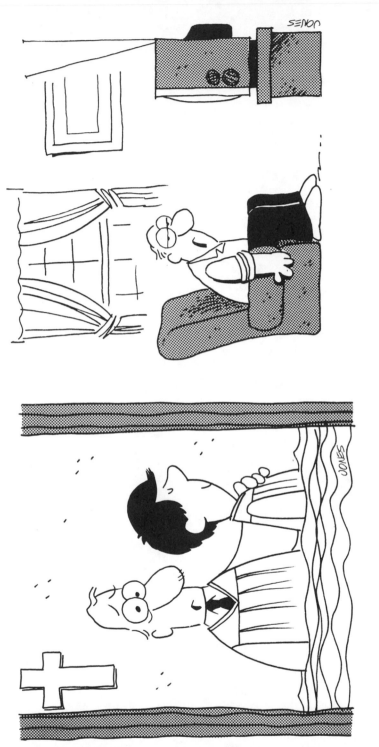

"WHY IS IT NO TV EVANGELISTS ARE BALD?"

"MISERY IS A HOLE IN YOUR WADERS!"

"WHEN IT'S TIME FOR THE OFFERING, I STICK THIS IN FRONT OF HIM. LAST WEEK I GOT FIVE DOLLARS!"

"DON'T BOTHER ME . . . I'M LOOKING FOR THE VERSE THAT SAYS IT'S OK FOR ME TO BORROW THE CAR."

"MISERY IS A HOLE IN YOUR WADERS!"

"WHY IS IT NO TV EVANGELISTS ARE BALD?"

"YES, IT IS FUN JUST TO SIT AND WATCH THE FIRE . . . BUT I KIND OF MISS SEEING COMMERCIALS!"

"I REALIZE THIS IS A YOUTH SERVICE . . . BUT I THINK IT'S GOING A BIT TOO FAR TO TAKE UP THE OFFERING IN FRISBEES!"

"I REALIZE THIS IS A YOUTH SERVICE . . . BUT I THINK IT'S GOING A BIT TOO FAR TO TAKE UP THE OFFERING IN FRISBEES!"

"YES, IT IS FUN JUST TO SIT AND WATCH THE FIRE . . . BUT I KIND OF MISS SEEING COMMERCIALS!"